AF278404

GOLDEN STREETCAR

March / April 2019

Volume I, Issue I

ANGELS FLIGHT BOOKS

ANGELS FLIGHT BOOKS

ISBN: 978-1-7337848-0-1

Director: Kareem Tayyar
Book design by: Karen Mao
Cover design by: Haley Wisniewski

www.angelsflightbooks.com

From the Director:

Why another literary magazine, when there already are so many? The only answer I can provide is that I don't think there can ever be too many forums for good poetry. Especially in the United States, a place brimming with more great poets than at any previous time in its history. I can only hope, as this first issue of Golden Streetcar launches, that Walt Whitman might take a break from celebrating the mysteries of Eternity long enough to bless this endeavor, and these poets, and the worlds they have birthed by putting pen to paper.

KAREEM TAYYAR

Contents

Suzanne Allen

CHER MONSIEUR

Grey is never strictly black and white, so
I need more sleep, less sunshine,
longer nights. These small boats just float

and float into every recurring lucidity we
ever share. I like the patchwork sails best,
don't you? We could fashion one from

our midnights. It would hold the wind
and push some wooden vessel off
over twilight's edge, as in movies. Say

it would. Say there's a reason for all this
bliss, for our secret languages, for
they are the captured wind itself.

Joan Bauer

DOROTHEA LANGE:
TRAINING THE EYE

From age seven, she would walk with a limp.
Dorothea, born in Hoboken.
No treatment in 1902 for polio:
        no choice but to accept
the pain, the hoof-like foot.

* * *

She crossed the Hudson by ferry for school,
PS 62 on Hester Street with tenement children
so hungry
for learning, they intimidated her.
        So she ignored school,
but trained her eye: strolling past
the storefront synagogues,
the Yiddish theatres,
        to the bars, pool halls of the Bowery,
then on to Wadleigh School for Girls.
Often truant,
she'd walk Harlem to Manhattan.

At graduation: *I want to be a photographer.*

* * *

For a time, she was Dorrie, portrait photographer
to the wealthy German Jews of San Francisco,
married with three children.
    But in 1932, she looked down
from her studio & saw desperate homeless men
in workman's caps & fedoras.

Among the first photos: White Angel Breadline.

* * *

In 1935, she met economist Paul Taylor
who was studying Mexican migration. He'd
taught himself

Spanish & learned how to ask unthreatening
questions,
like 'Where's the next town?'

He took Dorothea into the fields of Oroville.
He with his notebook, she with her camera.

Shacks, malnutrition, dysentery, scarlet fever, &
the armed men
who patrolled the migrant camps for the growers.
They fell in love
                    watching each other work,
divorced their spouses, married. From then, she
would live in Berkeley near the rose garden & the
university among the New Dealers & Marxists.

Officially, she was taking photos
for the government
& she'd tell migrants in the field:

I'm working for the President.

* * *

A rainy February day. 1936. Lange was alone
driving Highway 101 when she saw the road
sign:

PEA-PICKERS CAMP She drove on, then
turned back.

A freezing rain had ruined the crop. The mi-
grants stranded & starving.

The woman, Florence Thompson, was 32.
Seven children.
A haggard & careworn face.
Her children huddled,
hiding behind her.

Florence stares warily—into the distance.

Dorothea gave two photos
to an editor who contacted
the government & emergency
food saved the families.

Migrant Mother

The face of the Depression. On a 32 cent stamp.

A SLIVER OF LIGHT

for Roy DeCarava (1919 - 2009)

He began with sidewalk chalk art, encouraged
by his Jamaican single mother,

found his way to the WPA, Cooper Union,
the army,
but then, the turn from painting to the camera.

A Guggenheim & then Sweet Fly Paper of Life
with Langston Hughes,
not the 'punch-punch' shot,
but subtle poignancy. He worked without
assistants, developed his own film,
photographed exactly

what he found & never tried to 'brighten'
darkness, but deepened it using the softest paper
he could find.

Studies of Billie Holiday, Miles Davis, Coltrane,
& homage to everyday Harlem life: a man sitting

on a stoop, empty plates & catsup bottles,
brick walls,
stickball, tenement hallways, *hallways I grew up in.*

In 'Graduation,' a young lady bathed in light
walks between a trash-strewn street & vacant lot

toward a dim-lit billboard (for a Chevy Bel Air).
But is she looking at the billboard? Or moving on

despite the shadows poised to block her path.
Yet we say: 'I've seen this girl, I know her.'

DeCarava would say:
A sliver of light on the grating,
that's my hope, my optimism.

John Brantingham

END SONG

The only secret you need to know
to walk above the High Sierra tree line
is slow silence. Look down on the pine
trees, breathe, and allow yourself to go
the speed your body wants. Listen to pika
calling to each other, the final songs
of animals dying of heat. They will be gone
in the next summer or perhaps they may
last a few years, but take the time anyway
to listen to their voices as you refill
your body with air, as you stare out across
a hundred miles of mountains
in the dropping day
at a moment that might be the end of all
and everything. Listen to this song of loss.

AT 68

You can't even pat your dog
and not think about
that last "good girl" whispered
into her ear as the poison courses,
a raging muddy stream
after a flood. Your plan—
ask Doc to leave enough
in the syringe to give
yourself a good poke.

You watch your friend's daughter
bury her guinea pig who lived
years beyond expectation
on her love. She creates a grave
that makes death acquire symmetry—
a complex simplicity
of tree, leaf and rock,
a triumph of grief.

You're obsessed with Van Cliburn,
his gracious Texas drawl,
as he accepts his prize

in 1958 in Moscow where hope
lives in the massive chords
of Tchaikovsky's first piano concerto,
flows through rivulets of passion,
meanders and meditates
along romantic interludes,
dances with grin and scythe,
vodka and vole, towards
that last note of grace—
a whimper that ends
with a bang.

BLUE PLATE SPECIAL

Jim Harrison stepped aside and let Haruki
Murakami walk into the diner before him. Jim
only had one eye and ran into Haruki when they
both tried to enter the Bad Ass Diner at the same
time in Grand Marais, Michigan. Murakami
looked through Harrison, sat down at the
counter, and mumbled that solitude was his forte.
Jim took his place at the counter and
immediately fixated on the massive and
irresistible hind quarters of Darlene, the Bad
Ass's waitress. Darlene turned, coffee pot in
hand, and asked if they wanted a cup of Joe. Jim,
who took his coffee black, said he'd have a cup,
but asked for cream so he could watch her
backside when she turned to retrieve the milk
pitcher. Haruki raised a finger and Darlene
approached. You are the chrysalis of my sister,
he said, or my mother, or myself as a woman.
Darlene, Jim bellowed, I'll take the meatloaf with
mashed potatoes and gravy. Darlene barked the
order to the kitchen.

Haruki pulled from his coat pocket a large calico cat who told him that she is his mother turned feline by a mushroom cloud in Hiroshima. Haruki smiled, My job is solitude, he told her and sipped from a glass of water. Darlene appeared with Jim's dinner. Jesus Christ, Jim said, it's all blue—the meatloaf, the potatoes, the gravy—all blue! It's the Blue Plate Special, said Darlene. Murakami gently caressed the cat. They danced awkwardly to Debussy's Claire de Lune. I love you, mom, Haruki said, and twirled her around. Get me a bowl of hot buttered cheerleaders, cried Jim, grabbed Darlene, and jitterbugged wildly to Mexican reggae music. They bumped rumps till dawn.

Judith Alexander Brice

DAUGHTER-IN-LAW

She is not in the kitchen,
doesn't stand by the spice rack
she gave me last Christmas,
those spices that I use almost daily:

yesterday, the piquant barbecue salt to season
my special pork loin in apple cider
which I simmered with perfection
in our puffing pressure cooker—
the day earlier, the cinnamon and clove mix
which I chose to magic a pot roast—

as those sumptuous flavors wafted
to our living room, where she used to sit
in the velvet rocking chair while
reading her novel du jour,
oblivious to the hockey game
my husband and son razzed about,
got crazed about.

But these nights, the rocking chair
doesn't creak, the still air, now life-bereft,

silent of her daffodil voice.
The house is empty now,
no scent of years traversed before,
no hint of her tiny hands to pat the dog,
caress a heaving shoulder, a crying arm.

The guest double bed upstairs
has become a single once again.
The steps only groan
when my husband or I ascend to sleep.

IT IS FALL NOW,
ALMOST FROST,

(after William Carlos Williams)

And I drive by the pear tree
on Lake Grove Road—

You remember—

the one I wrote

about, and next to it
this year, its two babies,

nearly as big as it.
Imagine, all three

and pregnant now
with juicy pears

so full and rosyplump
they can't hold

on, not now, when
there are so many

more to come, ripe—
ready

to ring the trees around
and dot the grass with

luscious taste, so many
I almost turn the car

and stop, wonder
if the couple who

live in the trailer house
would mind...

would forgive me
if I pause, leave a note

to say:
they were delicious

so sweet
and so cold—

got crazed about.

THIS LAND

This land of Tanzanite and the Kilimanjaro.
This land of the Zambezi and the Victoria Falls.
This land.
The home of Mandela and Nyerere.
This Land of Kwame Nkrumah.
This land of the White and the Blue Nile.
This land of the Maasai Mara
and the wildebeests.
This land of the Great Migration.

This land of splendors.
This land of fear.
This land of frustration, intimidation,
and incarceration.

This land of cinnamon
and the cloves of Zanzibar.
This land of the music of the Congo and the
rage of the Kalashnikov.

In this land I have seen graves grow and flower.
In this land I plant my seeds of hope.
In this land I will toil until those seeds grow,
Or until I die.

HILI TAIFA

Hili bara la tanzanite na Kilimanjaro
Hili bara la Zambezi na Maporomko ya Victoria
Makao ya Mandela na Nyerere
Hili bara la Kwame Nkuruma
Hili bara la Mto Nile
Hili bara la Masai Mara na nyumbu

Hili bara lenye maajabu ya kuvutia
Hili bara la waoga
Hili bara lenye masaibu, vitisho na utekaji

Hili bara lenye mdarasini na mikarafuu
ya Zanzibari
Hili bara leneye sauti muziki ya Congo na
kishindo cha bunduki

Katika bara hili nimeona makaburi yakichanua
kama maua
Katika bara hili ninapanda mbegu ya matumaini
Katika bara hili nitapambana hadi mbegu
hiyo iote
Au hadi kufa

ONE DAY

One day,
What life has hidden from you,
Death will teach you.
What joy has kept from you.
Pain will reveal to you.

SIKU MOJA

Kile ambacho kimefichwa na maisha
Kifo kitakuvumbilia
Kile ambacho kimefichwa na furaha
Maumivu yatakuvumbulia

Keisha Cosand

THE PIANIST'S ORGASM

If you could have looked in the window,
you would have seen a young woman
sitting blindfolded at a black grand piano.
Sitting is not the right word for what she is doing.
She is playing with such force
that her body convulses and contorts.
If you had walked through the French doors of
the balcony,
you would have heard sounds
that would have moved
through your whole body
and lifted your soul out of your skin.
When the final note explodes
and slowly dissipates out the doors,
past the cliff, across the water,
off the edge of the sky
toward its long travel through space and time,
you would have seen the woman freeze,
put her hands in her lap,
sit still for a moment,

remove the blindfold
and walk out of the room
as if nothing had happened.

MILKWEED FOR MONARCHS

The Monarchs are feasting in the season.
For the first time, I don't care about the
Milkweed's sacrifice. The striped monsters,
in all their glory, eat and eat.

They are starting to make their move.
One old brother paves the way
across the vast expanse of lawn.
A green desert. Toward the tree.

It seems an impossible journey.
In misunderstanding, my daughter lifts him
And gently places him back on the milk branch.
How frustrated that brother must be.

I hear him curse,
"Dammit, girl! I am running on lost time!"
Again, he retraces the trail,
hoping she isn't watching.
On, the Monarchs march to a
new kind of branch—
the kind that can hold a chrysalis.

HEAVY CIRCLES

At the Norton Simon
near Old Town Pasadena,
We walk toward the moderns.
My eyes drift
toward a Kandinsky.
"Heavy Circles."
I see outer space
bright planets
eclipsing each other—
A crowded universe
crashing in on itself.
My seven year-old
sees bubbles—
heavy bright and floating.

Donna Hilbert

BURIED

A half-dozen kittens flat on the grass,
the first thing I saw from the car, one Sunday
when you drove me home from mass—
dead kittens arrayed across my dad's Dichondra.
I screamed, cried, carried on. I was seventeen.

You were twenty and soon returned to school
where you wrote daily notes on air-mail paper
about how it bothered you, my tears
over cats I barely knew. Something must be
wrong with me, you said, so much easy weeping.

I don't remember who wielded the shovel
that day, or when I stopped crying,
or where, exactly, everything was buried.

MAD MAX

Max keeps staring from the
back of the classroom.
I know he's drawing me as he looks
down at his paper,
then looks back up, down, up.
Today before class,
we passed each other in the hallway.
Max didn't suck up like another
student might have.
He just looked straight through me as if
he'd never seen me before.

In his first essay, Max wrote about how
all the kids in high school were fucking assholes.
I told him I liked his voice.
"Yeah," was all he said,
before he snatched his paper back.

The other students are in groups right now
while Max draws.
I should probably make him join them,
but I can't imagine Max joining anything.

I hope he's a good artist.
I hope he's damn good.
I hope when Max stares like he does,
he sees Van Gogh's café terrace,
Picasso's old guitarist,
Magritte's green apple.

I can't imagine him at a job interview
in a suit and tie.
I can't imagine him with a wife and children.

I hope the other students in here treat him better
than the ones in high school did.
I hope Max never pays a mortgage
or sends out Christmas cards.
And most of all, I hope he never,
ever, ever, ever, when he sees me
coming down the hallway,
stops and says hello.

JUST LIKE HEAVEN

"As a kid in Bulgaria," you say,
"there was a battery shortage,
so I could never play my tapes."

The Cure is at the Hollywood Bowl—
it's your first time seeing them.

A girl pulls a baggy out
of her purse, snorts some coke.
Everyone else takes selfies.

I grab your hand and spin you
around—I don't mention I prefer the deeper

cuts from this album—which I bought
with my allowance in 7th grade—

because you're mouthing
all the lyrics now.

When the song ends,
the girl dips back in her baggy.

People take more selfies.

We finish off a $2
bottle of wine we bought for $38.

Michael Miller

OFRENDA

for John Gardiner (1947 - 2017)

When we met, you were thirty-two steps ahead of
me on the hill that only slopes one way,
those gone before you

having tossed their words, their madnesses down
onto your shoulders as you carried them higher—
the workshop founded in the 1960s and so many
conversations about Kerouac and codeine

now forgotten by so many,
your randy tiger of a voice
booming them awake again for the younger poets

Saturday afternoons at the library, your yellowed
pulp magazines providing epigraphs
as you whittled

rants about Bush, poachers, the Internet—
all of us half-polite in the children's space.

Dear clown,

teacher, jester who sweetened so much anger,
I dreamed last night that we all hoisted
your own words and trudged

up that hill ourselves, the top uncertain but our
burning still
to let nothing drop below us. Up those cliffs,
those smashed coyote drags that turned
celestial in your poems,
we left the drivers below
who buzzed over crosswalks

and let Laguna stay beautiful
and crippled as you knew it—
even the drivers, now that we realized,
fragile enough to be someone's brothers.
We shouldered your words because they can only
rest on shoulders now, your voice

too far gone to call them back for revision.
They will spin in place if the stars' axles

will hold them. We should take this,

I suppose, as our blessing,
the gnarled cliffs that point
up instead of down—
the angle tilting our chins toward

what is higher, toward where wonder begins
when we've exhausted sand and sediment,
all our best maybe in sight.

Kelly Moffett

BELIEF

There are many windows where you live and you
open them all. The traffic-soot seeps into your
clothes, your skin. Daily, you wear the same bra
and feel the street dirt on your breasts. You see
what appears to be the same bird on Str. Andrei
Șaguna again and again with the rust-red collar
like a faded sun. It is the bird that seems to fear
you the most. It flees as soon as you arrive. You
think of the pigeon-handlers and how they paint
their birds different colors to tell them apart in
the sky. You think of the Tibetan word, day-pa,
which means confidence or trust but what could
be translated as faith and you repeat day-pa, day-
pa, day-pa until it becomes a mantra or a song.
No one saves us but ourselves. A woman told you
this. She now lives in a cabin in Appalachia and
sells garlic and lavender satchels and
home-spun brooms. So far from you now. The
canal is particularly shallow today. You have
nowhere to go. No reason not to stay and you
know the bird will return as soon as you part.
You know this like you know faith, which is

always somewhere behind a closed door but that you mark like a bird in order to distinguish it from others. You move on, since that seems the most natural thing to do, and you see life play out in the space you left behind as clearly as a memory. Where a bird returns to no one.

THE MARCH MARKETS

A man hands me dried lavender, his daughter
gives catkins, his wife five yellow tulips. There
is an early spring in in my hand I can't make
sense of—like the dead cockroaches in the very
clean apartment or the woman who lost her
groceries on the street then lost her life to
a very fast cab. Any of us could be hit by
anything. Love, too, might find a way to be
what it isn't. A casualty. I tell this to the students.
They all nod, so it must be true. A girl with
ribbons woven into her long braids hands me
a bag of potatoes. From others, I receive thirteen
daffodils, two bunches of lettuce, a lone iris in
plastic, a jar of honey, a wooden carving of
a dragonfly on a shoestring. I take all I am given
and pay all that I am asked. I wonder if this is
the woman I have been fighting to become or
if this is another version of the woman I have
always been. Then it's morning again. A full sky.
Church bells. The long skirt on the woman
passing me onions. Give me anything, I tell her.
I will take it.

LADY IN WAITING

She seems she wants to be certain
of something on the bench near Chios
Lake. Her eyes are on her phone. She
reminds me of the woman with a
cittern on her lap and a sealed letter
in her hand in Vermeer's The Love
Letter. Either the man has texted back
or he has not. But the woman seems
unable to see this as an answer.
He has not seen it, she thinks. Or he
is waiting until he has thought of
something witty to say. He's busy.
He will text back soon. She cannot
imagine the man not loving her so
she cannot look away, since the pain
will not ease until she sees his reply.
So she texts again. This time something
breezy like a warm day near the lake—
would be better with you and surely
the man will see this and feel special
and will want to give a reply. Perhaps
he will even stop what he is doing
and she will look up and the man
will be there with something small

in his hand like a daisy and then she
could put the phone away and they will
sit there together beside Chios Lake
and watch ducklings trail their mother
and feel a slight breeze off the water
and know how lucky they are to be
there on a good day in a good moment.
So the woman looks up but there is no
man with a flower, no easing of the chest,
no vibration in her hand that says it's
okay, that she is someone special and
worthy of a reply. Her whole life she
has been taught not to depend on men
to make her feel worthy and when she is
out with her friends or her mother,
they joke about women who need
men in their lives, but still she sits
with a hope so large in her chest
a nuthatch could pass through.

FEATURED POET:

Faith Shearin

The first Faith Shearin poem I ever read was "Fields", in Garrison Keillor's *Good Poems, American Places* anthology. I was, for lack of a better word, enchanted, the way one always is upon discovering an artist whose voice immediately beautifies and enriches the reader's world. While I could discuss the ways that Shearin's work extends the confessional lyricism of Anne Sexton, or even the way it is possessed of a prophetic voice similar to that of Leonard Cohen, the truth is that this still feels as if I am undervaluing her talents. Indeed, while she may be working within a lyric tradition that goes back centuries, to at least the French troubadours, the truth is that it is also a fact that there is no one else in American Poetry, past or present, quite able to conjure the type of earthly grace that she is able to in her work. She is, simply put, as good a poet as I have ever had the pleasure to read, with a rare optimism and joy threaded into her voice that one finds so rarely in modern literature.

With the recent release of her newest collection of poems, *Darwin's Daughter*, out now from Stephen F. Austin State University Press, Faith was gracious enough to discuss, among other topics, the poets who have inspired her, the role that poetry has played in her daily life, and the music that she turns to whenever she is in need of joy.

INTERVIEW

Do you remember the first poem you ever loved? What was it? And why do you think it moved you in such a meaningful way?

The very first poems I loved were the Mother Goose nursery rhymes my paternal grandmother read to me. I was pleased by the sound they made and I liked to recite them for her friends, in her garden, where she smoked and drank Pepsi from tiny cups; I liked to recite them inside her dark, brick house near the two scowling oval portraits of her parents, Jasper and Martha.

By age 10 I'd found Whitman's "O Captain, My Captain" and Edna St. Vincent Millay's "Childhood is the Kingdom Where Nobody Dies", both of them well crafted and emotionally powerful. The first poems I connected with in high school were James Wright's "A Blessing", Anne Sexton's "Her Kind", and Gary Snyder's "Four Poems for Robin." In each case, there was some revelation for the speaker that was both surprising and true. I remember sitting in my high school English classroom while Wright broke into blossom, and Sexton compared herself to a witch, and Snyder, sleeping in the open, remembered Robin.

Who are the poets whose work you continue to return to these days? What is it about these writers that has inspired such a sustained appreciation in you of their work?

A few of the poets I return to frequently are: Dorianne Laux, Elizabeth Bishop, Thomas Lux, Mark Doty, Adrienne Rich, Ellen Bass, Erin Belieu, Susan Mitchell, W.S. Merwin, Terrance Hayes, Louise Gluck, George Bilgere, Marie Howe, and Nick Flynn. In their best poems all these poets pay careful attention to language and imagery and sound; they unpack the human condition. When Adrienne Rich dives into the wreck, or Thomas Lux writes about the cherries he never ate in his childhood refrigerator, or Gerard Manley Hopkins asks Margaret if she is grieving over GoldenGrove unleaving, or W.S. Merwin asks what was the matter with love on his shoulder, or Mark Doty tells a bigot what kingdom he, as a gay man, will inherit, I am transfixed.

Are there a few artists in other mediums— music, painting, fiction, film—whose work has informed your own work as a poet? How has their work impacted your own?

The other women in my family are visual artists and my first fellowship, at the Fine Arts Work Center in Provincetown, was among painters and sculptors. Once, talking to my sister, who is a sculptor and potter, we realized we were working with the same idea; she was throwing plates and bowls with little maps inside, to memories on the island where we grew up, and I was writing a series of poems which gave directions to the past; in some cases her visual directions and my verbal ones were nearly identical. I am moved by the photographs of Sally Mann and Diane Arbus, and by the paintings of Frida Kahlo and Marc Chagall, which explore the emotional realm through imagery in a way that is quite close to poetry. Some of Woody Allen's early movies ask questions I am grappling with today. (Observations like "I feel that life is divided between the horrible and the miserable…" still resonate for me.) So do Spalding Gray's revelations about sex and death. For thirty years I have driven around in my car listening to musicians like Joni Mitchell, Bob Dylan, Greg Brown, Leonard Cohen, and Lyle Lovett, who have written lyrics that also succeed as poetry. I am moved by color and image and sound, by moments when verbal skill meets emotional honesty.

In much of your work, there seems to be a strain of magic realism that connects your poetry to novelists like Gabriel Garcia Marquez and Isabel Allende. A poem like "Fields", for instance, where the narrator articulates the dual worlds she simultaneously inhabits—the world of the modern, defined by trips to the post office and nights at the opera; and the pastoral,

mystic world of her ancestors, which is
informed by an abiding faith in moon cycles
and old wives' tales—reads like a story by
Borges. Can you discuss the origins of this
particular motif in your poetry, and why it
is an aesthetic reservoir from which you are
able to draw so much narrative power?

Very early in college I found the work of people
like Isabel Allende and Gabriel Garcia Marquez:
writers who wrote of the visible as well as the
invisible, of ghosts and creatures with wings;
their use of magical realism certainly influenced
me. When I was young I worked as a high school
English teacher and I taught the Rosa short story
"The Third Bank of the River" in which a father
rows away from his family, in a boat, to live on
a nearby shore, where he can be glimpsed but
not spoken to, or known. The metaphor was so
emotionally powerful, my students often wept
when speaking of what it meant to them. If I
think about it, that same magical impulse is in
Frida Kahlo and Chagall paintings: she becomes
a deer full of arrows, or he flies on the back of a
chicken. A writing exercise I liked to give
beginning college students was to look into a
photograph and imagine what was unseen, just

outside the edges of the photo. In another exercise I asked them to look at popcorn and imagine what it could be, but was not. Frida allows us to understand her pain differently when she places her head on the body of a deer; Chagall gives us a new way to think about happiness when he rides with his new bride on the back of a chicken. In magical realism, the world we see gives way to the world we cannot see, which is also the world inside ourselves.

Whenever I teach your poems, I am consistently struck by how accessible my students find it. They often mention in class discussions how they feel as if your narrators have gathered their listeners around a campfire and casually begun to tell their stories. Is poetic accessibility something that you are conscious of striving for?

Growing up I had uncles who sat on front porches, telling stories. My Uncle Bill, in particular, was a big man who made me laugh. I was aware, as a child, of waiting for him to come into a room. I am, in many ways, a failed short story writer. It was the first genre I loved.

(I actually began my MFA in fiction, and switched genres halfway through.) The world of literature and storytelling should belong to everyone; inside good stories are the metaphors that help us make meaning of our lives. My husband was a student at Princeton University and once, visiting him in college, I was not allowed inside their library because I did not have a Princeton ID. I'm still angry about being excluded from those books. Poetry that is purposefully elusive frustrates me; it makes me feel stupid and shut out. So I suppose I am devoted to crafting poems that are easy to enter, transparent.

I am fascinated by how regularly myth figures into your poetry. In "Lancelot" for instance, which retells that most famous of Arthurian tales in a voice that echoes The Gospel According to Mark; or "Argos", which focuses on Odysseus' ever-loyal dog, who bears silent witness to his owner's extended absence with a heartbreaking-ly moving patience. What is it about the narratives that form the core of Greek and Western European myths that continue to speak to you?

I am a huge fan of fairy tales and myths; I love the underworld in Greek mythology with its pomegranate trees and its river of forgetfulness; I love the magic in Camelot: the way Lancelot was raised under water by The Lady of the Lake and Merlin knew the names of the knights of the Round Table before they were born; I love the stories of people sleeping for one hundred years, and getting lost in forests, of mirrors speaking and cursed spinning wheels. I love creation myths and flood myths. These stories are meaningful to me because they are full of universal worries and jealousies and desires. This must be why we give them to children: as early maps.

I don't know of an American poet who writes more beautifully about the experiences of marriage and motherhood. How have these two facets of your life informed your poetry?

My early poetry was especially concerned with marriage and motherhood because these were some of my most powerful early adult experiences. My love for my husband and daughter startled me, made me feel confused and vulnerable. Now that I am nearly fifty I feel the poems turning their attention towards loss and grief, towards endings. I live in a world increasingly inhabited by the ghosts of people and animals who have departed; I stand beside the ghost of my younger self. My favorite poems allow me to discover something while I am writing them, something which was hidden from me, something I knew but did not consciously acknowledge. Sex and love and death are realms in which I make constant discoveries.

Is there a poet whose work you particularly love that you feel is deserving of more recognition? Who? And what is it about their poetry that resonates with you?

I am aware of how easy it is to be marginalized in poetry, which is itself a marginalized genre. My friends who became professors, and enjoy giving readings, and attending conferences, have fared better than people like me who taught high school and had a series of odd jobs before becoming, more or less, a housewife who writes in her car. I have read so many poems by high school students that I find more moving than most poetry in *The New Yorker* or *Best American Poetry*. The poems written by kids when

when I was a poet in the schools were raw,
emotionally honest, and devoid of posturing,
or rarified references. Jim Daniels and George
Bilgere are examples of poets who identify as
working class and plain spoken; they do not
receive much attention but have written some
gorgeous, powerful poems.

**What is the last novel you read that made
you fall in love with literature all over
again?**

When I brought home Donna Tartt's first novel
The Secret History I stayed up all night reading it;
the novel is both murder mystery and
literary masterpiece; it brings together the world
of Classics with some fundamental questions
about human nature. Mostly, though, I have been
transported by children's literature: *The
Magician's Nephew*, *The Hobbit*, *Nurse
Mathilda*, *A Tree Grows in Brooklyn*.

**What film have you seen more times than
any other? How come?**

I have watched *The Graduate* more times than I
can count; Benjamin Braddock's confusion after

graduating from college is something I can relate to; I think I am still struggling to find a comfortable place in the adult world. I love the scene in which Benjamin is dressed in diving gear, peering through his mask at his parents and their friends, the way he floats aimlessly around a swimming pool, the scene in which he is advised to pursue plastics.

What is the greatest concert you have ever seen? What was it about the performance that has stuck with you?

I saw Lyle Lovett perform with his Big Band at the Telluride Music Festival when I was in my early 20s; he had just married Julia Roberts, which turned out to be a mistake, but he was flushed with excitement and he sang "If I Had a Boat." Maybe you know the song? "And if I had a boat/ I'd go out on the ocean/ and if I had a pony/ I'd ride him on my boat/ And we could all together/ Go out on the ocean/ I said me upon my pony on my boat." I was young and there were mountains all around and I had been camping with a lot of interesting people and this beautiful nonsense song spoke to me of desire and longing, of wanting a pony and a boat at the same time; Lovett created this delightful image of riding a pony on a boat on the ocean, something laughable and fantastic and wonderful. He had big hair and a long, crooked face and he had *words*.

Poems by Faith Shearin

All three of these poems were originally published in Darwin's Daughter, Stephen F. Austin State University Press, 2018

EMILY DICKINSON, CALLED BACK

Emily lived fifteen years beside West Cemetery,
watching those solemn
processions towards silence and,
just before she died,

she wrote: Dear Cousins, called back.
Her casket was carried by six Irish workmen and,
following her instructions, they circled

her flower garden, walked through a horse barn,
took a grassy path through fields to a grave

lined with evergreen boughs, inside an iron fence;
she was called back the way children are
called home

in the evenings, dusk falling over rooftops,
wagons and baseball bats abandoned in the
grass, called back

the way dogs are called back from forests, their
noses pointed towards doorways.

You know this like you know faith,
which is always somewhere behind
a closed door but that you mark
like a bird in order to distinguish it from others.
You move on,
since that seems the most natural thing to do,
and you see life play out in the space
you left behind as clearly as a memory.
Where a bird returns to no one.

GUINEVERE, PRAYING

Gone was the table as round as a compass
and gone, too, the wizard, Merlin,
who climbed the Pine of Barenton,
hand over hand, up a ladder of branches,
had a great revelation, and never returned
to the mortal world again. After the last battle
at Camlann, King Arthur was placed in a barge
and sailed to the Isle of Avalon where
he drifted amid mists and apples,
tended by his sister, and Guinevere
went to live in a convent
near Stonehenge, love's fire behind her.
On her knees, hands clasped, she spent
the rest of her life in prayer: apologizing
for desire, Camelot flickering in her mind.
A black habit hid her hair and her room
was made of stone, her bed stiff. She was
bent, like my grandmother at the end,
over regret. Sometimes,
in dreams, Lancelot galloped past her:
his sword sharp, night burning.

ANNE SEXTON'S FINAL DRIVE

On the night she did not die Anne Sexton
wore a red dress and waded
into the Charles River,

waist-high in water, washing down pills
with a thermos of milk;
this turned out to be a rehearsal

for the evening, months later, when
she removed her rings and slipped into

her mother's fur coat. It was October
in Boston—sharp air, deepening leaves—

and Anne drank Vodka in her garage,
inside her vintage Cougar, driving

towards the end of the world, her radio playing.

Dave Newman

15 OF ANYTHING

After a week in Mexico
doing a job he hates
selling industrial parts
to other Americans
living in Mexico
who work for companies
that pay Mexicans
          almost nothing
to work on assembly lines

my brother comes back to the States
and stays up all night drinking
while his wife sleeps
and his kids sleep
and he finishes beer after beer
until Mexico
is an afterthought
until selling
is as distant
as a factory
in Juarez.

The next morning
as my brother wakes
from a horrible night's sleep
in a hungover ball
on the couch
covered in a blanket
he bought for 7 bucks
at the airport

his young son tiptoes downstairs
and steps into the kitchen
looking for a juice
and some cereal.

He eyes the empty beer bottles
a small forest
of brown glass trees
which apparently
grew overnight
on the counter
by the sink

and he says
"Who drinks 15 of anything?"

and all of us in the world
who know

answer, quietly, "Adults."

SEEK

It starts with a beer in a paper cup
in the backyard of someone's house.
It starts with getting punched
or learning to punch someone else.
It starts with what you want to be
and ends with what you refuse.
It starts with the Holy Bible.
It starts with creation, starts with light.
It starts with water, it ends with dirt.
It starts with whatever you remember:
gloriousness and terribleness.
It ends with forgiveness. It always
ends with forgiveness unless it ends
with rejection, unless you crumble.
It starts anywhere and ends
exactly how you want it to end.

When I am loving Walt Whitman
too much I try to remember
that towards the end of his life
when rumors of his gayness
abounded, Whitman countered
by bragging that he'd fathered
children all over the South.

Never forget your own hate.
Never forget your own fears.

The world keeps spinning.

Run so it's not running
but faster than running.
        Try backwards.

Shannon Phillips

IN ARABIC, THE MOON IS MASCULINE.

"Surely, that can't be right,"
I tell my professor.

The moon is a goddess,
la luna; she is needed,

like a mother.
"There is hope," my professor says.

"In poetry,
the moon can switch gender."

Slippery words
suit me.

In poetry,
sometimes I need

a masculine-she;
other times,

a feminine-he
is needed.

In poetry,
words wet

the inside of my mouth,
like fat from a spit,

for a feast
under the moon.

BARSTOW TO VEGAS

for my father

I was 10 and he was 30 when he finished the 400-mile
dirt route from Barstow to Vegas,
on a yellow dirt-bike
with thousands of other noisy wasps.

He had to be peeled from the handlebars, hands
in semi-permanent curl, the perfect scoop for
burst-bag Doritos,
a pile fallen from a tailgate celebration.

Goggles off, those orange triangles complimented
the pale cut-outs of his eyes,
dust thick as a shadow on his face.

SOLITAIRE

My thoughts
keep me company
in ways
I wish others would

CHOOSE

We can be nice
or
we can be lovers

Lloyd Schwartz

THE WORLD
(from the Tarot deck)

Let's begin in the beginning, or at the end—
aren't they really the same?
Creation/Revelation.
A snake chewing its own tail,
circumscribing a naked lady clutching
stiff twin staffs, like giant
pencils (to scribble whose long story?).
Glazed trophy heads—a dazed (or dazzled?) lion,
a blowhard bull, a glaring eagle, and one benign
human face—surround her; sounding her, staring
her down. But stark naked,

she has arisen, and she's stepping out.

Off to her writing desk? Her haven? Her raven?
Do revelations lie in store?
Is this how she conceives *The World*?
The round earth's imagined corners:
trumpets, strumpets, numberless infinities;
demons mangled, angels strangled, angles
tangled; from lowly ground, forms arising,
dissolving; from dearth, hearth, birth;

then—*burn,*
batter, blow—death, woe
(with every grace, abundant tyrannies).

Look, daybreak again—or twilight.
The snake bites! Repent. Pardon. Mourn.

Scott Silsbe

THE LONELY VOLUNTEERS

"I don't know why we do it.
We must be crazy."
- Richard Hugo

There isn't any real point in questioning why we
do it. It's a lonely craft, for sure. It alienates the
most social of us. But it's some sort of odd
compulsion, I suppose, to put down words like
this, try to articulate the thing.

Richard—I think of you and your fine poems
all about Montana and Italy, bars and loneliness
and your friends. I think that your friends called
you "Dick," but you died when I was just four
years old, so we two never met, we never became
friends, so I think that I'll stick to Richard.

I'm not sure what I would say to you if I had
the chance. I suppose that I'd thank you for your
poems. It's funny, isn't it, how we feel a gratitude
for the work of others?

But your poems have enriched my life—that's
the way I think about it. You once wrote, "You
have to be silly to write poems at all." And I can
see that. It's ridiculous. So is writing a poem to a
dead man who'll never read it. I don't know why
I do it. I must be crazy. But maybe, it's something
very human—this urge to communicate with
someone who isn't around anymore. And maybe
it's one of the things we do that is odd,
but endearing.

I don't know for certain, Richard, but I think
that maybe, you might understand me when I
say that lately I find it difficult to tune into the
nightly news report, to learn of the many horrors
human beings are capable of these days. I want
to scream obscenities at the television, but I know
that wouldn't help.
And I don't know what would help.

So I switch the machine off. And I pull your
books down off the shelf, sit with you a while.
And you make me want to try harder. To get
better. To be better. And to accomplish
something with this, the only life I know that
I will ever have. I feel lonely because of your
poems. And I thank you for that.

Clifton Snider

AT THE GRAVE OF EDVARD AND NINA GRIEG
—TROLDHAUGEN, NORWAY

Their names are carved large,
sidewise
bold and crude
in a dolmen
embedded in a cliff-sized rock
surrounded by Norwegian birch,
white and pink flowers
in woods inhabited by trolls
and tourists,—
it faces the sprawling lake
with its islands
covered evergreen
in the exact spot
where the sun hit
on an afternoon
and the composer of Peer Gynt
said, "When I die,
put me there."

Clemens Starck

ANOTHER DAY

Three blue jays (two Steller's and a scrub jay)
not frequently seen together
are perched on the branches of a dead mimosa
jutting out from the overgrown thicket of
flowering quince,
a tangle of green dotted with pink.
Three blue jays
on a blustery morning in March . . .

Almost eighty now, an octogenarian,
I should have some words of wisdom to impart.
But it turns out the infirmities and indignities
of old age—a tin can tied to a dog's tail,
as Yeats says—
are not necessarily
conducive to wisdom.

Now chickadees, nuthatches, finches and juncos
emerge from the thicket,

and together with me and the jays
they celebrate.

Our various forms of twittering, squawking and
hopping about
attest to our being alive on the planet
at least for another day.

STARTING FROM LISBON

Writing to me from a sidewalk café in Lisbon,
my friend, an airline pilot,
is waiting, he says,
for two refurbished engines to be installed
on the 767 he flies for Aramco
before taking the plane back to Brazil.

Could this be the beginning of a poem?
I wonder, and ask myself,
If it were, where would it go from there?

Fernando Pessoa, the Portuguese poet
who divided himself into multiple personalities,
assigning to each its own heteronym
and using his own name only for one of them,
never married,
earned his living as a
"commercial correspondent,"
drank heavily and died at 47.

How one thing leads to another, and
what *this* has to do with that,
is not always apparent at first.
One day you wake up with a frog in your throat,

next thing you know
the doctor says you've got six months to live,
if you're lucky.

And I haven't even mentioned Camoëns,
the 500 English archers
on the field at Aljubarrota,
the cathedral-toppling earthquake of 1755
and the sinking of the *Lusitania* . . .

Thomas Thomas

A CASUAL READ

it was just a
casual read

I don't think
you knew,
Kim died
last year

a message
from one
friend to
another

a stale message
six months old

about a girl
I thought I
loved once

and in my car
a CD plays
Led Zeppelin

and I was a
little jealous
because you
thought Plant
was cute

and thirty years later
I spent a whole trip home
from work talking to you

and it was like
thirty years had
never passed

and you were
just like I
remembered

and I know why
all the girls I liked
friends and lover

were the type that
weren't afraid to tell me
exactly how they felt

the type that would
tell me to go to hell
faster than *I love you*

and the call was over
and I later heard
you had cancer

and the news was old news
but time is not old

the news of your death is today
and today I put the
phone down on our last
conversation

and this very moment
we are sitting in
your bedroom

listening to
Stairway to Heaven

Lynne Thompson

LIGHT OF A DARK BLACK NIGHT

when doves cry, despair
prickling their wings, crisp
air surrounding while I am

down here among sinners
and each tear and struggle
falls back in my eyes.

(Repeat, but

vanity is no less
false than a surface.)

Nothing's like this cupboard
of want. Nothing's prescient
in the way everyone speaks of.

Trust nothing
but doves under the eaves,
inviolate on their journeys.

It's this simple:
yearning never yields & zero
is always the ultimate number.

TRANSLUCENCE

in memoriam, Deborah Digges

I last saw her not long before
she fell or leapt. She spoke softly
and without surrender and we,
unwary, suspected nothing.

Even if we'd known everything,
nothing is all we would have known.
What continues to haunt—why?
she was neither friend nor colleague—

is that she was a woman balancing
a paper plate full of pasta and curly
endive, pretending the fall evening
might last & last; who was, I thought,

a little shy but not withholding. What
remains is her complexion, translucent,
a shimmer of light reflecting through,
drawing us in as though we'd entered

a private sanctorum, uninvited, a salt-
and-brink-of place where we couldn't
stay. Without concern, I turned and
walked off. Didn't say goodbye, good luck.

The next evening, as she read her poems,
she seemed serene, a mystery gilding
her smile. She stepped out of her heels
and, with grace, crossed the proscenium.

Robert Walicki

EVERYTHING IS FINE

We walk slowly through the glass doors,
astonished as children at the didgeridoos,
the Buddha bowls of dull brass
that sing like clear rivers.

A grey-haired woman palms a spell book
and dusts the floors with her dress.
Walking upstairs at Journeys of Life Books,
I let the psychic take my hand for 60 dollars,

while you drift through racks of cards.
I'm not supposed to say anything negative she says,
but I can see you're unhappy.
Her fingers trail my palm,
count the lines of my life.
"You're going to live long,
but many health problems",

she says. This psychic's not what I expected.
No head wrap or tassels on her dress.
She's clad in Keds and a Joan Jett t- shirt,

says, *Nothing is ever locked in,* and that
our lives are rivers. It all depends on how you swim.

I want to ask her, "What if I'm drowning?"
But decide I don't want to know how it will end.
If the toaster will fall
and break my toe next Tuesday,
If the road will glaze over this February,
send my car

through the guard rails,
wheels spinning in the air.
Instead, I leave Mira's hands
and the bad news upstairs,
dream of the river I'm supposed to have,
the tide and current of the Discover Card bill,

the school taxes we can't afford.
Down in the gift shop, I watch
you finger through cards with suns and glistening
angels on them.
I want to say, "Let me see your hands"
and "I'll tell you everything."
But we fold into a tired hug,

mute the wordless language of the married,
as in, *I'm hungry and let's go.*
Are you ready, and *everything is fine.*

BOXES

At this age, you never think about
how it will end,
Besides it might not happen,
and you'll have to
put on those week-old jeans again,
dried stiff with ditch mud,

30 years of 7am's.
The blue exhaustion of Monday
and it's overheated coffee.
No one would fault you
if you have a shot and a beer
for Sal who got smacked

in the head with the excavator.
After all, it's almost 3 o' clock
and the drunk operator is sorry
and 6 months will find him
sliding pipe inside pipe again,
sharing the dug-out earth

with you. *An inch every four foot drop*
means in a few feet we'll be deep enough
for boxes, he says, So we can get outta here,

so these walls don't collapse.
I stare up at the scaled-back earth,
crumbling walls and drop to my knees,
lay the pipe down
and wait for the walls to come down around us

Cave-in boxes he called them,
swallowing up all that blue sky,
this dieseled air, this momentary light

PERSONAL

SWM ISO SWF for GF, LTR or BFF. Must be
21 again and standing in your mother's kitchen,
far enough from your father's oxygen tank to
swear it was ocean. Window must have a view
of weeds and the neighbor's screeching cats.
Pics are optional though must be able to point
out constellations lying in open fields in the dark.
Bonus points If you've ever been torn apart
by a Mahler symphony the day you held a mirror
under your grandmother's breath for answers.

if it's yes to sunsets that look like they're on fire,
to the psychic who touched you with her electric
hands, called you one of us, yes to those broken
lifeguard chairs on the beach reading The Shack
at midnight under moonlight. If you were here,
anywhere when the sound of the tide was like a
thousand faucets bursting at your feet,
that was me.
I was out there calling and calling your name.

Rafael Zepeda

TEST PILOT

I'm watching a movie I've never seen before
with Clark Gable,
Spencer Tracy and Myrna Loy.
Gable is a hot test pilot and Tracy
is his smart-ass mechanic.

Earlier this afternoon,
I fell with a ladder that was
propped up on my boat,
the ladder sliding down with me on it,
and I cut my chin up,
splashing blood all over
a brand new white shirt—
so I ended up with seven stitches.

My wife told me,
"You have to quit climbing ladders.
You're too damn old."
But as I lie on the couch and watch the movie,
I think about all of the good movies
I haven't seen,
all of the good stories I haven't read.

I've seen and read a lot of them at my age,
and I keep seeing more and more good movies,
reading more good stories
when I'm lucky.

Sometimes Brando or Bogart might be in a film
that I've never seen before,
that I watch until two or three in the morning,
or some book's character might
sail the green oceans.

I love watching these people
argue and cuss and dance across
the screen and the page.
They're like old friends that I haven't even met,
if that makes any sense.

This banged-up chin just gives me a good reason
to lie around and watch Gable
flying as a test pilot,
Tracy giving him sage advice,
until both of them spin down to earth
to crash in flames,
to make Myrna Loy weep at the loss
of both of them.

When this movie's s done it's three o'clock
and I go to bed
happy that my fall didn't end up as bad
as Gable's and Tracy's did.

THE WAITING

It had been a long time since I'd gone
into the ocean
to swim or catch a wave
and it was August
and the monsoon had rolled in
from Mexico
so it was muggy and my shirt was wet
and sticking to my skin.
I just had to go into the water.
I'd been taking one dog or another of my dogs
down to the beach and the water
to run and chase after the ball
for thirty years or so.
My current golden always ran like a cheetah
chasing the ball two or three times,
to then put her belly down on the wet sand
and let the wave wash under her
so that she cooled herself off,
dog air conditioning.
I realized one day that
she'd been getting her exercise,
whereas I'd only been walking up
and down the beach for a mile,
not getting much exercise at all.

Besides that, I hadn't been in water for months.
I'd always loved to go into the ocean
so that it could suck the sin and the poison,
which there was plenty of, out of me.
Until ten years before,
I'd been going down to the beach
and jumping in the water,
wetsuit or no wetsuit, waves or no waves,
for three decades.
I'd gotten bad sick so I'd been
unable to jump in the ocean
for many years.
When I'd gotten well,
I'd grown lazy and out of the habit of diving in
and getting wet in the ocean,
which had been one of my few good habits.
So I left my dog at home one day
and went down to the beach
where I'd always gone,
where there were very few people
and only an occasional good wave,
especially when the Santa Ana winds, a swell,
and the tide happened to come together.
I put my fins on and swam out to
beyond the surf-line

and floated there watching for
the glint of the sun
off of any swell in the slate-blue sea,
glad to be there,
if just for the waiting.

AUTHOR BIOGRAPHIES

SUZANNE ALLEN is an interior designer turned writing instructor whose poems have appeared in print and online publications such as *Carnival, Cider Press Review, Pearl, Spillway, Spot Lit, Tears in the Fence, Writing in a Woman's Voice, Not a Muse*—Haven Books, *Strangers in Paris*—Tightrope Books, and in *Villanelles*—Knopf. She has two chapbooks: *verisimilitude* (CorruptPress), and *Little Threats* (Picture Show Press.)

JOAN E. BAUER is the author of *The Almost Sound of Drowning* (Main Street Rag, 2008). With Judith Robinson and Sankar Roy, she co-edited the award-winning international anthology, *Only the Sea Keeps: Poetry of the Tsunami* (Bayeux Arts and Rupa & Co, 2005). In 2007, she won the Earle Birney Poetry Prize from *Prism International*. In 2018, she was a finalist for the John Ciardi Poetry Prize from BkMk Press. For some years, she worked as a teacher and counselor and now divides her time between Venice, CA and Pittsburgh, PA, where she co-hosts and curates the Hemingway's

Summer Poetry Series (www.hemingwayspoetry-series.blogspot.com).

JOHN BRANTINGHAM is Sequoia and Kings Canyon National Park's first poet laureate. His work has been featured in hundreds of magazines and *The Best Small Fictions 2016*. He has ten books of poetry and fiction, including *The L.A. Fiction Anthology* (Red Hen Press) and *A Sublime and Tragic Dance* (Cholla Needles Press). He teaches at Mt. San Antonio College.

CHARLES W. BRICE is a retired psychoanalyst and is the author of *Flashcuts Out of Chaos* (WordTech Editions, 2016) and *Mnemosyne's Hand* (WordTech Editions, 2018). His poetry has been nominated for the Best of the Net anthology and a Pushcart Prize and has appeared in *The Atlanta Review, Hawaii Review, The Main Street Rag, Chiron Review, Fifth Wednesday Journal, SLAB, The Paterson Literary Review, Muddy River Poetry Review and elsewhere*.

JUDITH ALEXANDER BRICE, a retired Pittsburgh psychiatrist, has had poems published in many on-line and print journals and newspapers including *The Paterson Literary Review*, *VoxPopuli.com*, *The Pittsburgh Post-Gazette*, *Versewrights.com*, and *Annals of Internal Medicine*, among others. Her first book, *Renditions in a Palette*, appeared in 2013. Her second book, *Overhead From Longing*, has just hit the shelves. One of her poems, *Mourning Calls*, was set to music by Tony Manfredonia, and the composition for voice, English Horn, Flute, Violin, Harp and Cello as performed by the Pittsburgh Tuesday Musical Club can be heard at https://www.manfredoniamusic.com/mourning-calls.

OCHAM COLLINS is a Lecturer of Creative Writing and Teaching Methods in Literature at St. Augustine University in Tanzania. He holds a Bachelor's Degree in Literature from The Catholic University of Eastern Africa and a Master's Degree in Literature from the University of Nairobi.

KEISHA COSAND teaches literature, composition, and creative writing at Golden West College in Huntington Beach, California. She lives with her husband, two young daughters, and yellow lab, Numan.

DONNA HILBERT'S latest book is *Gravity: New & Selected Poems* (Tebot Bach, 2018). Her work is widely anthologized, most recently in *Poetry of Presence*, (Grayson Books, 2017). She is a monthly contributor to the online poetry journal *Verse-Virtual*. She writes and leads private workshops in Long Beach, California, where she makes her home.
Learn more at www.donnahilbert.com.

CLINT MARGRAVE is the author of *Salute the Wreckage* (2016) and *The Early Death of Men* (2012), both published by NYQ Books. His work has appeared or is forthcoming in *The Threepenny Review*, *New York Quarterly*, *The Writer's Almanac*, *Rattle*, *Cimarron Review*, *Verse Daily*, *The American Journal of Poetry*, *Word Riot*, and *Ambit* (UK), among others.
He lives in Los Angeles, CA.

MICHAEL MILLER is a former *Los Angeles Times* journalist and the author of three books of poetry: *College Town* (Tebot Bach, 2010), *The First Thing Mastered* (Tebot Bach, 2013) and *Angels in Seven* (Moon Tide Press, 2016). A cofounder of Moon Tide Press, he ran the poetry series for years at the Muckenthaler Cultural Center and has been nominated twice for the Pushcart Prize. He currently lives in Los Angeles and teaches English at Our Lady of Lourdes Parish School.

KELLY MOFFETT has three collections of poetry and a chapbook. Her work has appeared in journals such as *Rattle, Colorado Review, Laurel Review*, and *Cincinnati Review*. She acts as Director of Graduate Studies and Coordinator of Creative Writing at Northern Kentucky University.

DAVE NEWMAN is the author of six books, including *Please Don't Shoot Anyone Tonight* (Broken River Books, forthcoming 2018), the novella *Sammy Drinks Canned Beer* (White Gorilla Press, forthcoming 2018), *The Poem Factory* (White Gorilla Press, 2015), the novels *Raymond*

Carver Will Not Raise Our Children (Writers Tribe 2012) and *Two Small Birds* (Writers Tribe Books, 2014), and the collection *The Slaughterhouse Poems* (White Gorilla Press, 2013), named one of the best books of the year by L Magazine. Winner of numerous awards, including the Andre Dubus Novella Prize, he lives in Trafford, PA, the last town in the Electric Valley, with his wife, the writer Lori Jakiela, and their two children. He works in medical research, serving elders.

SHANNON PHILLIPS is a freelance editor and aspiring translator (Arabic-English) who earned her MFA in Creative Writing from California State University, Long Beach. She is also the founding editor of Picture Show Press. *Body Parts*, her most recent chapbook, was published by dancing girl press in 2017.

CHAN PLETT is a poet and copywriter in Seattle, Washington. Their writing has been featured in *Magpie Magazine*, *Dum Dum Zine*, and other DIY literary zines and journals. Titles by this author include *Honey Surviving Oil* and the forthcoming micro-poem collection *Death Rattles*.

LLOYD SCHWARTZ is the Frederick S. Troy Professor of English and teaches in the MFA program at UMass Boston. A Pulitzer Prize-winning arts critic who appears regularly on NPR's *Fresh Air*, he is also a leading authority on the poet Elizabeth Bishop. His poems have been selected for the Pushcart Prize, *The Best American Poetry*, and *The Best of the Best American Poetry*. His latest poetry collection is *Little Kisses* (U of Chicago Press). He is the Poet Laureate of Somerville, Massachusetts.

FAITH SHEARIN is the author of *The Owl Question* (May Swenson Award), *The Empty House, Moving the Piano, Telling the Bees, Orpheus, Turning* (Dogfish Poetry Prize), and, most recently, *Darwin's Daughter*. Her work has been read aloud on *The Writer's Almanac* and included in Ted Kooser's *American Life in Poetry*. She has received awards from the National Endowment for the Arts, The Barbara Deming Memorial Fund, and The Fine Arts Work Center in Provincetown. She lives in Massachusetts.

SCOTT SILSBE was born in Detroit and grew up down the river from there. He now lives in Pittsburgh. His poems have appeared in numerous periodicals and have been collected in three books: *Unattended Fire* (2012), *The River Underneath the City* (2013), and *Muskrat Friday Dinner* (2017). He is also an assistant editor at Low Ghost Press.

CLIFTON SNIDER, faculty emeritus at California State University Long Beach, is the internationally-celebrated author of eleven books of poetry, including *Moonman: New and Selected Poems* and *The Beatle Bump*. He has published four novels, most recently, *The Plymouth Papers*, his first historical novel. A Jungian/Queer literary critic, his book, *The Stuff That Dreams Are Made On*, was published in 1991. He is the inaugural recipient of the Lorde-Whitman Award from OUT LOUD: A Cultural Evolution (July 2018).

CLEMENS STARCK is a Princeton dropout, a former merchant seaman, a retired union carpenter and construction foreman, and the author of six books of poems—including the award-winning *Journeyman's Wages* (1995). The others are: *Studying Russian on Company Time* (1999), *China Basin* (2002), *Traveling Incognito* (2004), *Rembrandt, Chainsaw* (2011) and *Old Dogs, New Tricks* (2016). A book of his Collected Poems, *Cathedrals & Parking Lots* was recently published. A widower, he has three grown children and lives outside of Dallas in the foothills of the Coast Range in Western Oregon. (www.clemstarck.com)

THOMAS R. THOMAS publishes the small press Arroyo Seco Press. Publications include Carnival, Chiron Review, and Silver Birch Press. His books are *Scorpio, Five Lines, Climbing Eternity, in which the world is turned upside down, and the art of invisibility*.

In 2018, LYNNE THOMPSON won the Marsh Hawk Press Poetry Prize for her manuscript, *Fretwork*, which will be published in 2019. She also authored *Start With a Small Guitar* (What Books Press, 2013) and *Beg No Pardon* (Perugia Press, 2007), winner of the Great Lakes

Colleges Association's New Writers Award. New work appears or is forthcoming in *Barrow Street, The New England Review, Ecotone* and *Poetry*. Thompson is Reviews and Essays Editor of the literary journal, *Spillway*.

ROBERT WALICKI'S work has appeared in a number of publications, and he currently has two chapbooks published, including *A Room Full of Trees*. His next collection, *Black Angels*, is forthcoming from Six Gallery Press.

RAFAEL ZEPEDA is a Professor of English at California State University, Long Beach. His previous books include *Horse Medicine & Other Stories, Tao Driver* and *Selected Poems, The Wichita Poems, The Yellow Ford of Texas,* and *The Durango Poems*. His poems and stories have appeared in many anthologies and magazines. He has received a National Endowment of the Arts Creative Writing Fellowship in Fiction, a California Artists' Fellowship, and a Poets, Essayists and Novelists Syndicated Fiction Award.

CPSIA information can be obtained
at www.ICGtesting.com
Printed in the USA
BVHW030309080920
588160BV00004B/22